My Monster.. "The Brother"

Hound dog

Knuckle Head

Princess

Pumpkin

AuthorHouse™
1663 Liberty Drive
Bloomington, IN 47403
www.authorhouse.com
Phone: 833-262-8899

Because of the dynamic nature of the Internet, any web addresses or links contained in
this book may have changed since publication and may no longer be valid. The views
expressed in this work are solely those of the author and do not necessarily reflect the views
of the publisher, and the publisher hereby disclaims any responsibility for them.

Any people depicted in stock imagery provided by Getty Images are models,
and such images are being used for illustrative purposes only.
Certain stock imagery © Getty Images.

This book is printed on acid-free paper.

ISBN: 978-1-4567-0019-5 (sc)
ISBN: 978-1-4817-1488-4 (e)

Print information available on the last page.

Published by AuthorHouse 03/14/2024

authorHOUSE

We have a monster that lives in our
house, when things go wrong we blame
the monster

One day mommy made a beautiful cake
and when it was ready to serve someone
had ate half ... The monster was to blame.

Another time Daddy was building a new cabinet and couldn't find his tools....The monster was to blame!

My sisters and I never play with
the monster, sometimes this makes the
monster mad and he breaks things.

After dinner everyone wanted
chocolate ice cream, but we had vanilla
instead because that's what the
monster wanted.

Another time we were going to go to the movies and couldn't go because the monster got sick, we were very mad at the monster.

Mommy bought me some cowyboy
boots but I never got to wear
them because the monster took them!

We have a dog that likes to play
catch ... He sometimes hides.
because he's afraid of the monster.

One day my mommy told me that
if I was nice to the monster, the
monster would be nice to me.

One day at school a big bully
was picking on me.

When the monster saw the bully picking on me, the monster scared him away.

When I went home I made the monster
some vanilla ice cream and I
thanked him for what he had done....

...the monsters face started to
change and I found out I had
a brother and not a monster!

Now I play with my brother and we have lots of fun, but every now and then the monster still shows up!

Printed in the United States
by Baker & Taylor Publisher Services